ARE YOU RETIRED OR RETIRING SOON?

ARE YOU RETIRED OR RETIRING SOON?

*Enhance Your Retirement Income
By Trading Stocks*

by
Warner Noel Aboutet

Order this book online at www.trafford.com
or email orders@trafford.com

Most Trafford titles are also available at major online book retailers.

Printed in Victoria, BC, Canada.

ISBN: 978-1-4269-2011-0 (sc)
ISBN: 978-1-4269-2012-7 (dj)

Library of Congress Control Number: 2009939962

*Our mission is to efficiently provide the world's finest, most comprehensive book publishing
service, enabling every author to experience success. To find out how to publish your
book, your way, and have it available worldwide, visit us online at www.trafford.com*

Trafford rev. 11/05/2009

 www.trafford.com

North America & international
toll-free: 1 888 232 4444 (USA & Canada)
phone: 250 383 6864 ♦ fax: 812 355 4082

Contents

PREFACE

I wrote and published this book to coincide with my retirement at the age of 60. I thought that this was a great way to start my retirement to keep myself busy for the first few months of retired life! More importantly, this book was written to share my trading stock experience with retirees, the soon-to-be retired and all others who were wondering if when and how they could afford to retire after the global economic recession of the 21st century. I decided to retire because I have confident that I could live comfortably based on the retirement pensions from the government and from a LIF (Life Income Fund) which is a special Registered Retirement Income Fund (RRIF), plus the supplemental income generated by trading stocks within my self-directed Registered Retirement Saving Plan (RRSP).

I am a Canadian. Throughout this book I had made references to Canada's retirement income such as the Canada Pension Plan (CPP) and Old Age Security (OAS), and the terminologies for registered retirement plans may not be the same between the two countries. U.S. readers can interpret the Canada's retirement income with the ones that are similar in the States; for example, the CPP vs. the U.S. Retirement Insurance Benefits (RIB), and the employer-sponsored group Registered Retirement Savings Plan (RRSP) vs. the U.S. 401(k). Despite these subtle differences, the two countries share a lot of things in common, and the global economic recession has affected the lives of citizens of both countries.

If you were retired or retiring soon, do you have doubts that your retirement plan portfolios are sufficient to provide you with a good retirement income? In this book, I have shared with you my experience on how to enhance my retirement income by trading stocks.

To Karen, for putting up with me in our relationship; may your life be as happy as can be.

To Felix, Cindy, and Stephanie for their editorial assistance in shaping this book

CHAPTER ONE

A Nightmare in the Stock Market

I started to write this book in March 2009, hopefully to have it published in December 2009; at such time I already have had executed my investment rescue plan for about a year to turnaround my sinking portfolios. As a matter of fact, the plan is more than just an investment rescue plan. It is a plan for paving the final stretch of the road to retirement. The investment rescue plan is really my retirement income plan to support my retirement; I am depending on the money made from this plan to provide a decent retirement income.

Six months before my retirement, in February 2009, I submitted a Retirement Application to the Canada Pension Plan (CPP), with the expectation of receiving the pension benefits from CPP starting in September of 2009. In February 2009, I informed my employer of the intention to retire by the end of August 2009. At the same time, I submitted an application to Sun Life Financial to transfer my equity in the Defined Contribution Pension Plan (DCPP) to the Sun Life Financial Group Retirement Income Plan LIF (Life Income Fund), which is really a special Registered Retirement Income Fund (RRIF), so that I would start receiving payments beginning in September of 2009.

As the economic downturn began in mid-2007, and the economic freefall from

September 2008 to March 2009 started the worst recession since the Great Depression, and as I was approaching the age of sixty, there were a number of reasons that drive me to make the decision to take early retirement.

If I didn't make this decision to take early retirement at sixty, I could continue to work until the age of sixty five or older, to make up for the loss in equity due to the market meltdown. This is what most financial planners and investment advisers are saying: retirement for most baby boomers is being put on hold because of the current state of the economy. The common belief of the average retirement age is now changed from 62 to 67.

If I was to retire at the age of 65 instead of 60, would I still need to implement the investment rescue plan now? The answer is "yes". I would still do exactly the same thing to rescue my retirement investment, and then about six months before my 65th birthday, I would do the same preparation like I did for my 60th birthday. I would still need the retirement income plan to provide a supplemental income; without it, my retirement income from the government and from the LIF would be below the poverty line. What I need is a supplemental income from the "payout" of my retirement investment. The "payout" is generated by trading stocks.

Due to the loss of equity in the stock markets, some baby boomers just couldn't afford to retire after this global economic recession triggered by the domino effects of the credit crisis, because most of their investments for retirement are tied to equities in the markets. The market values of their investments have decreased significantly. They could not have a good "harvest" from the investments they have made during their entire work-life. They have to stay put and hope that the markets will rebound, and their equities might recover the hefty loss in the next few years. The common message from financial planners and investment advisers is, "Trust us, and if you stay put, the market will bounce back in the future..." At the time when this book was being written, nobody knows if the recovery would be a "V", or a "W" shape. Between the optimistic and the pessimistic forecasts, it's more likely that the recovery road is not without bumps and turns, and it will take until 2010 at the earliest to see a global gross domestic product (GDP) recovery.

Towards the end of 2008, my total loss from three different portfolios was about 25% calculated year-over-year. Maybe it was not as big a loss compared with the major market indexes; but it was still the biggest year-over-year loss of my lifetime equity investment.

If you are retired or a soon-to-be retiree, is your loss situation similar to mine? Please read on and then decide what your next step is.

I had determined to implement my investment rescue plan without the help of any financial advisers; and to do so, I needed to put more time and effort into it. This might be one of the excuses for me to decide to retire at sixty. Another reason was that my wife had already retired two years ago.

Without an employment income after retiring, I need to lower some of my expectations and live within my means. I cannot survive with just the money coming from the CPP and the Group Retirement Income Plan LIF; therefore I need to supplement these incomes by another source. The investment rescue plan is really my retirement income plan to support my retirement; I am depending on the money made from this plan to provide a decent retirement income. I am calling this plan an investment rescue plan because I am taking control to stop my portfolios from sinking further. I am calling this plan a retirement income plan because it is my primary source of income to support my livelihood after retirement; therefore, from now on, I am going to call this the Plan.

The Plan had been implemented since December of 2008, and was making a gain of $42,323 in *cash* after 9 months. This was a decent growth from a capital of approximately $95,400 (which is the average monthly balance of the cash portion in my portfolio) that I used to trade stocks. The stock trading technique described in this book could not guarantee you to become rich, but rather, the book emphasizes the importance of having an investment strategy of your own for your future retirement.

The main theme of this book is to show you how I manage my single portfolio in today's market, and use this single portfolio to trade stocks. It is not as difficult as it sounds. It is not as risky as most people think. As a matter of fact, I feel very safe to manage my portfolio this way because I am a baby boomer and I would not risk my life-time retirement savings if I am not comfortable with what I am doing. After I have implemented my Plan, I could sleep better every night and not worry about how the market will perform the next morning!

If you are not as old as I am, or you are not a baby boomer, my suggestion to you is to start an investment plan for your retirement as early as possible. If you already have an investment portfolio, and are not happy with your financial adviser, why not try to manage your own portfolio? It is no use not looking at your monthly statement of your investment portfolios and hoping that your loss will recover in the next few years. You need a plan to take control of your own investments. If you trade stocks, you are more active and watchful on your portfolios and you might achieve higher gains.

These days, most companies are offering pension benefits to employees a Defined Contribution Pension Plan (DCPP) instead of a Defined Benefit Pension Plan (DBPP); and it is up to the employees to manage their own investment in the DCPP. In today's economy, workers are not 100% guaranteed to receive their pension benefits from a DBPP if the company went bankrupt. As a result of this economic recession, some big companies' pension funds for the DBPP are underfunded because they were invested in equities that have suffered losses; this means that their employees' pension benefits will be affected if these companies went bankrupt. For workers who do not have DBPP or DCPP, then relying just on CPP and Old Age

Security (OAS) is absolutely not an option at all if they do not have a different or separate personal retirement plan on the sideline. We all need a 'Plan B' or 'Plan C' for preparing for our retirement years.

If you are in your 40's or 50's, and you have some equity build up in your investment portfolios, and you are not too happy with your current financial advisers, or you have currently lost your jobs because of the economy, and trying to make ends meet by having two part-time jobs, or you already have tapped into your RRSP to draw money out. Why not take control of your financial future and try trading stocks? Just start with some small and careful steps initially and slowly build up your confidence; there is always a learning curve in doing everything.

If you are a stay-at-home mom and you have a few hours to spare during the day, you could venture into this and build up your financial future. If you have a spousal RRSP that is invested in a very conservative and safe way like guaranteed investment certificate

(GIC), discuss with your spouse first before getting into trading stocks during the daytime while your kids are at school. Investment management can start right at home! You can do it if you are willing to try.

But I have a word of advice for the younger working people. You can consider using my method of managing your portfolios, but please do not give up your daytime job and do it full-time. This society requires a workforce to fulfill many needs. I do not like to see the workforce reduced if the younger generation starts to quit their jobs and just sit at home to trade stocks! I am taking early retirement because I have been working for thirty-six years since I left college, and I think it is time to take a break from my engineering profession and explore something different. My financial responsibility is much reduced now because my kids are no longer relying on my support, and therefore I can afford to take some calculated risks which I was not dare to take five or ten years ago.

CHAPTER TWO

Consolidation Of Different Accounts Into One Account

Many of us were quite happy to see the market took off between 2003 and 2007. The Dow Jones Industrial Average (DJIA) and the S&P/TSX Composite index (the main index of the Toronto Stock Exchange) were at their all time highs in the summer of 2008. We worried that the bubble might burst one day, but few people predicted that the market could fall off its cliff.

My niece's husband (Sam) warned me in August of 2007 that the financial sector would be in trouble due to the sub-prime mortgage situation. I followed his advice and sold the bank stocks in my holdings. But later in the year, the S&P/TSX regained its loss from the summer. I was sort of forgot about the warning and merrily continue to invest in the stock market.

In retrospect, I should have been more cautious after August 2007 or even better, sold everything and hold only cash. Many of us would like to turn back the clock and exit from the market. In 2008, my three portfolios were in a mix of mutual funds and stocks in approximately eighty per cent and the rest are in cash and mortgage. By year's end, my total loss in market value was about $100,000 due to market turmoil.

I did some hard thinking in the late fall of 2008, and came to the decision that I must change my strategy in investment from then on. The loss of twenty-five per cent year-over-year of my total portfolios is a wake-up call.

One of my three portfolios was in a Defined Contribution Pension Plan (DCPP) held in Sun Life Financial. The DCPP was a pension benefit provided by my employer who matched my contribution to the DCPP dollar-for-dollar up to a maximum of six per cent of my annual salary. Each employee who participated in the DCPP would manage his/her own portfolio. Although I had an absolute freedom of managing this plan, I had a limited choice from a *set menu* of several mutual funds in equity, money market, and guaranteed funds that were available for picking. After eight years in this Pension Plan, all the gain was wiped out by this global economic downfall.

My second portfolio was a Registered Retirement Savings Plan (RRSP) that was set up about six years ago and held in a small financial investment company. This portfolio consisted of mostly mutual funds and a small portion in money market. Again, at the end of 2008 all the gain from this account was wiped out.

My third portfolio that I am actively managing now is a self-directed RRSP which I had set up with a web-based discount broker. Before the stock market crash, this portfolio was in a mix of mutual funds, ETF and stocks, and a $35,000 mortgage for my house. The mistake I made in this portfolio was that I did not dedicate enough time to manage this self-directed RRSP. This is not good especially in a bear market or volatile market. Due to the stock market meltdown, I took a hefty loss in this self-directed RRSP.

These were the actions I took last year for preparation of my retirement and implementation of the Plan.

For the first portfolio, I transferred all the mutual funds into Money Market funds in December 2008. In preparing for retirement, I had submitted an application to Sun Life

Financial to transfer my equity in the Defined Contribution Pension Plan (DCPP) to a Group Retirement Income Plan Life Income Fund (LIF), so that I could start receiving withdrawal payments starting in September 2009.

My Plan for the second portfolio was to consolidate it into my self-directed RRSP. This sounded like a simple exercise, but it took six months (from June to November) to complete, due to some stupid things happened in the banking institutions. While I was waiting for the transfer, I did not hear or see anything from the receiving institution (in this case, it is the institution that holds my self-directed RRSP). I don't want to elaborate on what had happened, but all I would say is, do not assume that all the employees of banking institutions know what they are doing, and if you suspected that things were not happening as expected within a reasonable time frame, go and check out what's wrong because if the transfer did not take place due to some stupid backroom procedures, the banking or financial institutions always have their excuses.

By November of 2008, the consolidation was completed and I was determined to take control of my own investment; I began to actively manage my retirement investment!

CHAPTER THREE

Ready to Roll

Some time in 2008, I was watching CNN's Special Report on the economic recession. The program showed a retired teacher who had to come out of retirement and worked again after 4 years of retirement. This teacher said that his retirement income was reduced because his investment in mutual funds took a plunge in values.

My first portfolio that was held in Defined Contribution Pension Plan (DCPP) did not hold any mutual funds since the beginning of 2009. While I was still working for my employer during the last few months before retiring, I directed the contribution money to be invested into Money Market funds. Unfortunately the DCPP was a locked-in retirement pension plan and I could not consolidate 100% of the DCPP account assets with my self-directed RRSP. Therefore, I elected to transfer 100% of the money into Sun Life Financial's Retirement Income Plan Life Income Fund (LIF). After I had taken retirement in September, the remaining DCPP balance will be transferred into the LIF account. This account will provide me an annual withdrawal amount divided into twelve payments. Similar to the DCPP account, the LIF account requires the client to manage his/her own investment. I had chosen to invest into two Income Funds for the LIF account.

For my second RRSP portfolio, I had sold all the mutual funds except one after they were transferred to my self-directed RRSP. The reason I am still hanging on with the unsold mutual fund is because the loss would be too much if it was sold in today's market. Now, with the equity of the second RRSP portfolio consolidated into the self-directed RRSP, I can take control of my own investments!

Don't trust financial advisers! I have nothing against them. They have to make a living too. Most of them are good and very professional, despite sometimes we hear about some bad apples in the profession. Unfortunately, people do get burned because they put their money into the hands of some financiers or swindlers, like the cases of Bernie Madoff in the U.S. and Vincent Lacroix in Canada. Base on my own instinct, I do not believe that my best interests are being taken care of in the hands of financial advisers, and I believe that I can do better without them.

I remembered when I was in my early

fifties; I called a financial adviser and asked him if I could retire at age 55. After going through very briefly about my net assets on the phone, he told me bluntly that if I didn't have about a million dollars at that time, it was not likely that I could retire. I was quite disappointed, not because of my hope to retire at 55 was dashed. I was disappointed that he didn't offer much advice on the phone, or offer to sit down with me to work out something for me. He hinted that if I wanted to "retire comfortably", I need to have an asset of about $900,000.

Now I am 60, and I do not have $900,000 to support my retirement. However, I am more confident than ever that I could retire at my age. It does not matter that the economic recovery is still uncertain. It does not matter if the market trend is up or down, as long as the market opens everyday, I could have a fair chance to make some money. Forget about what the general opinion says that the average senior will have to postpone their retirement age later than 65. Here I am, poise to retire.

In this book, I am going to tell you how I can manage to do it. Hopefully, the same approach can be used by those who are willing to try.

CHAPTER FOUR

How to Make My Money Work for Me

In investment, we often come across some typical rules or advices for investors:

- Do your homework first before choosing a financial adviser.

- Ask questions to identify potential conflict of interests.
- Ask questions about risk factors.
- Check whether the fund firm's interest is aligned with yours.
- Check to see if the fund manager's interest is aligned with yours.

I do not need to follow the above advice, because in implementing my Plan, I do not need any financial adviser, I do not buy mutual funds and bonds, and the risk that I am dealing with can be minimized by adhering to the process that I will describe in the later chapters.

I have this self-directed RRSP portfolio to manage by myself. How do I make it work for me? I trade stocks only; I do not trade derivatives; and I do not trade bonds. Some people might say that trading options and using margins account will give them more leverage. I am not recommending these at all. I like to stick with a simple method, that is, just a no-margin stock trading account, because trading options requires observation (such as watch out for the expiry date) and margins account requires maintenance margin.

I do not think that the financial planners and investment advisers recommend investors to do what I am doing, that is, trading stocks. On the other hand, I see more and more TV commercials from on-line discount brokerage companies selling the advantages of electronic trading. One TV advertisement that I particularly like is the script in the Scotia iTRADE™ commercial; it emphasizes the main reasons why we should trade on-line.

It is understandable that financial planners and investment advisers prefer investors to put their savings in safer investments because the public in general likes to accept low risks investment products. That is why the investment planning and mutual fund industries are promoting products like fixed income and mutual funds. If they recommend their clients to trade stocks on their own, then they will not have the business from these clients.

I find that choosing a mutual fund to buy is not that easy. I'd rather pick stocks to invest in because I do not have to research about fees for front-end load, back-end load, purchase, redemption, management expense, etc. that mutual funds are charging the investors.

You might wonder why I trade stocks in my self-directed RRSP. Well, the short answer is, that's where I started to put my retirement investment in since the early eighties. Like any typical Canadian, if a person puts money into RRSP yearly to defer paying some of the income tax, he or she will end up with equity built-up within the RRSP, as long as it is invested safely and avoid losses that could wipe out the investment completely.

The government and most financial institutions encourage people to start preparing for their retirement by saving as early as possible. However, when it comes to investing, it seems that the average Joe is being left at the mercy of his own picking and the risks of making wrong decisions. Some people will tend to be very conservative and invest in GICs, while some will invest in riskier investment and financial instruments. A good example is investing in the Lehman Brothers Minibonds. Some investors who had lost their money in Lehman Brothers Minibonds complained that the fine prints were so difficult to understand.

First of all, I must proclaim that I am not an expert in stocks. I do not study and analyze stock charts in great details. I will explain how I trade stocks within my self-directed RRSP to make money.

My first RRSP account was opened in 1981. After five years, I consolidated that RRSP account into a self-directed RRSP account which was with a full service broker, and every time when I wanted to buy or sell a particular stock, I called my account executive who would execute the trade for me, with a commission fee charged to my account. I was not buying or selling very frequently, and I paid an annual fee for this account plus a rather high commission for every trade. I picked stocks without any particular criteria, and my trading pattern at that time was "buy and hold". I did not make a lot of gain, and I did not calculate exactly the growth percentage yearly. It survived the Black Monday, October 19, 1987. By 1989, this RRSP had a total worth of about $32,000 mainly through contributions into it.

In about the mid-90's, I switched the self-directed RRSP to a discount broker, and began to place buy or sell orders through the telephone and then later through internet access. The savings in the commissions per trade was substantial by using a discount broker, especially if the trading frequency was high. My trading pattern was still the same, and I gained some and lost some. It was a learning period for me.

Then beginning in the late 90's, my trading activity was restricted, and before every buy or sell order, I had to submit a request to trade to obtain approval through Email from the investment compliance department of the financial company where my wife was employed. I thought that this procedure was absurd, because my wife knew nothing about her company's trading; but I guessed this was a mandatory compliance rule for the employees and their spouses to follow.

Therefore my trading activity was very light for about seven years, and until June 2007 (my wife had retired from that company), I began to trade more frequently. Then in December of 2008, I decided to implement my Plan, and began to trade even more frequently, but not daily.

To implement my Plan, I buy big cap stocks listed in the TSX; I don't buy penny stocks. I very seldom trade U.S. stocks because of the fluctuations of the currency exchange rate. I have a list of ten to twenty big cap Canadian stocks (for example CM, TD, SU, RCI.B, CP, AGU, ABX, etc.) that I trade frequently.

I watch the business news on TV or listen to radio in the morning before the market opens, and find out how the market performed in Asia overnight, and how the London and European markets are performing in the U.K.

and European time zones. I watch the Dow Jones Industrial Average (DJIA) and the S&P (Standards and Poor) indexes futures in the U.S. markets. This is important because the TSX market follows the U.S. markets most of the time. I watch the TV business news channels like the BNN and CNBC and keep myself up-to-date of the latest news related to the market, for example, company reports on earnings, M&A (mergers and acquisitions), and economic data such as consumer confidence, new house sells, interest rates, GDP, unemployment, etc. All of the above provides information that could affect the opening of the market.

About an hour after the market has opened, I pick a stock that is in the sector which is "up" during the day. I buy at market price in quantity of 500 to 1,000. Sometimes, the market is flat and there is no obvious choice for a particular sector. If this was the case, I would look at the biggest winners and biggest losers to see if any of them were in my list. You might ask, "What is the right price to buy a stock?" I will expand this in the following chapter.

After I have bought a stock, I immediately put in a sell order for the same stock, with the sell price of $0.10 to $0.30 above the price I paid earlier. Sounds simple? Buy low; sell high (not that high really for my strategy). If you look at the historical price of any stock, the data will show the High, Low, and Close prices. The Close price is usually always above the Low price of the day. Therefore under the normal case, there are enough rooms between the intraday High and Low prices that I can trade a stock and make a profit when the timing to buy is right.

I can flip one or two stocks, or more each day. On average, if I made $250 a day, it would be $250 x 20 trading days in a month = $5000. From December 2008 to March 2009, the four months' average cash gain from trading was at a respectable figure of $5245 per month, while the market went through a terrible period and it tanked to the bottom on March 9, 2009. From April 2009 to August

2009, the five months' average cash gain from trading was $3,890. My nine months' (December 2008 to August 2009) average cash gain from trading was $4700 per month. Nine months of results may not be a strong evidence to prove that I could succeed in the long run. However, the results prove that I can make money by frequency trading in a "down market" (December 1, 2008 to March 9, 2009) and in an "up" market (March 10, 2009 to August 31, 2009).

In my self-directed RRSP account, I try to maintain 50% cash, and 50% equity. I don't want to expose too much by having too much stocks in the portfolio at the end of the day, especially in the volatility of today's market. Ironically, it is the volatility of the stock that I am taking advantage of during the trading day that provides me the opportunity to earn money. My strategy is: "Don't be greedy. Just try to earn $200 to $300 a day on the average".

You could ask, "What if the stock drops in price after I have bought it?" I hang on to it for one, two, or a few days until the price is above the Buy price. That is why my stock choice must be big cap stocks. They will likely go up again. Since I started frequent trading in December 2008, I do not have a single stock that I need to hang onto for a long period because of price drop. In my account, I am still stuck with two stocks that have dropped in value, but these two stocks were bought prior to starting of my Plan in December 2008.

Most of the time, I try to buy and sell off the same stocks at a profit within the same day. There were times that I sold off the stocks with a loss because I was not comfortable with their downward trend. Sometimes I sold the stocks at the same price that I bought them. But most of the time, the stocks were sold at a profit within the same day, or within several days.

It is a good feeling to not hold a large quantity of stocks in my portfolio at the end of the day, because the market conditions can change overnight, and when I wake up the next morning, there might be a load of bad economic news that can cause a weaker opening market, and the market values of the stocks in my portfolio could decrease. In the next morning, if I don't have the stocks, I can buy the stocks again near their intraday Low prices.

CHAPTER FIVE

What Skills Are Needed For Frequent Trading?

I mentioned in the previous chapter that I am not an expert in stocks. What I mean is I do not study stock chart in great details to analyze and predict the future direction of a stock is headed in. It must be helpful if one has the skill or knowledge to analyze different plots and charts, but I can manage without such technical analysis. I might look at the day, week, month, and year charts of the stocks if I was interested in buying them, just to see their movements in the day, week, month, or year.

However in general, I pay attention to the pulse of the market; I watch the business channels on TV (such as the CNBC, Bloomberg, and BNN) but not glued to it all day long; I read the business section of newspapers if it happened to be available and within my reach; and I scan the internet for news related to the market when I am using my PC.

Couple of years ago, my daughter Cindy gave me a satellite radio at Christmas. Now, my car radio is switched on with the Bloomberg Radio on Satellite while I am driving. My ears are now tuned to the news about the market and the economy, and anything related to them. It's a great way to learn day by day, a bit at a time, for an old guy like me.

If you are not comfortable to use a personal computer (PC), or use the internet at all, I am not going to write about how to learn such tricks. This is a skill you have to acquire by your own efforts. Ask a friend or a kid of yours who is savvy in PC to show you how to obtain access to an account with an on-line discount broker, and then learn how to place a buy or sell order.

After the market opens, I usually do not buy before 10 a.m.; I'd wait until the stock prices settle down. I look at the quotes of the stocks from my list after I have performed the login to get access into the on-line broker's website. During trading hours, the quote provides the instantaneous prices of the list of stocks being queried. I am not paying extra money to the discount broker to use the more advanced trading platform that provides live streaming data while the market is open. The advantage to use live streaming data is to be able to see level 2 quotes (for the "real" day-traders and brokers/dealers); however, the normal platform without live streaming data is good enough for me.

As I mentioned in the earlier chapter, I try to watch the news related to the pre-market conditions to see which sector will be "up" or "down". After the market has opened and the stock prices have settled down at around 10:30 a.m. EST, I will pick a stock in the sector which is "up", for example, the banking sector. In my list of stocks, I have the five major Canadian banks which are listed in a portfolio, and by a click of the "portfolio button" the quotes will be available for these five banks. I look at their quotes: the Day Low and Day High, Open, Last, Bid, Bid Size, Ask, Ask Size, Change, Ticker, and Volume.

If the market of the day is "up" and the banking sector is the leader to cause the market to advance, it is a buy opportunity of a bank stock of my choice. The question is: which bank stock I should pick. I look at the five quotes for the five banks, and compare their "Changes" (in prices compared with yesterday's Close prices). I compare which bank has the smallest or biggest "Change". In this example, if all five bank stocks are "up" on the day, then the "Changes" are all on the plus side. To decide which stock to buy, I would pick the stock that the Ask price is slightly above (or near) the Day Low, and I anticipate that the Ask price could move up later. After I decide to pick this particular bank stock, I will have to pick an entry point to buy the stock. While I am in the Quote page of this candidate stock, I will click the refresh button several times to look at the Bid, Bid Size, Ask, Ask Size, Last, Change, and Ticker symbol. These numbers and the Ticker symbol are likely to change every time when the page is refreshed; this indicates that the stock is actively traded.

As I have mentioned before, the trading platform that I am using does not provide me with live streaming data, therefore I need to click on the refresh button to get an instantaneous quote just every time when the refresh button is clicked. But this is good enough to provide me an indication of where the Bid and Ask prices are, and their respective

Sizes (this is the most commonly displayed level 1 quotation market data, the Best-Bid-Offer). If the Ask Size is much larger than the Bid Size, and the Ticker symbol is negative, then it is an indication that the sellers are eager to sell, and the stock might be trading in the downward trend at that point in time. On the other hand, if the Bid Size is much larger than the Ask Size, and the Ticker symbol is positive, then the indication is that the demand for the stock is high, and the stock is likely trading upwards at that point in time. In this case, I will select to buy the stock at the market price. As a matter of fact, I always buy a stock at the market price when I decide to buy.

Before I commit myself to buy the candidate stock, I might check the TSX index one more time to see if it was going up or down. If it was sliding down, I would hold off the buy and wait and see. If the index was still on an upward trend, then I would commit myself to buy. After I have put in the buy order, I will check the status of the buy order to see if it is filled. Thanks to electronic trading, the order will be filled within a few seconds. This is true when the stock is traded actively and Volume is high as indicated on the Quote page.

Now it is time to put in a sell order of the same bank stock that I have just bought. My target is to make a small profit. If I could make $300 a day, I am happy. Therefore, the sell order is to sell the bank stock (quantity of 1,000) at a sell price of $0.32 higher than the buy price (the $0.02 is sufficient to cover the commissions of $14 for both buy and sell orders). It's not that complicated compared with making the decision to buy the stock. The business of the day from hereon is to sell the shares before the closing bell. If the trading of that stock was upwards at that moment, the sell order would be filled within a few minutes.

Sometimes, the sell order might not be filled for half a day because the market's earlier gain is pared by news that affects the upward momentum. Later, I could change the sell order to lower my ask price by ten or fifteen cents just for the purpose of selling the stock before the market closes.

If the entry point of buying the stock is right, that is, the buy price and timing is right, the sell order will be filled within minutes if my ask price is not exceptionally too high above the price I paid for the stock. Sometimes, but not often, the stock market turns south after I have bought the stock and my sell order cannot be filled or partially filled at the end of the day. Well, I will keep the stock in my portfolio and try again the next day. Remember I said earlier that I only trade big cap stocks. This stock will trade above the price I paid for in the next day or next few days.

I usually do not average down when I am stuck with a particular stock, this being said, I sometimes take exception to this rule. A recent example was that I averaged down Barrick Gold (symbol ABX) because I saw a surge in gold price and I was stuck with a quantity of 500 shares that was bought at a higher price sometime ago, so I bought another 500 shares at a lower price. In doing this, I was able to unload the 1000 shares sooner. For beginners, it is better to keep it simple and do not use the average down technique.

In another scenario, if a company's stock opens with a drop in price, due to takeover of another company by this company, this might be a buying opportunity for both companies. I usually avoid reacting to such opportunities and stick to my rules to be conservative. These opportunities come and go very quickly. The gain could be very high if the timing is right and the takeover is a good move, but the risk associated with it is also high if the takeover bid failed to succeed.

During a trading day, you could have one or a few orders simultaneously or one at a time, depending on market conditions, your internet setup speed, the amount of available cash in your account, and your comfort level of handling multiple orders through electronic trading. If you are a newbie, you will pick up the skill or reach a comfort level as your trade frequency increases. Start with an order quantity of 500, one order at a time, and then increase it to 1,000 when you become more skilful. I like the quantity 500 and 1,000 because it is easy to calculate the gain when I sell the stock. For example, for a quantity of 1,000, if I sell the lot at $0.25 above the Buy price, I make $250 minus $14 (for commissions) = $236. If the lot size is 500, the profit is $125 minus $14 = $111.

I always trade the same stocks from my list of companies. I limit the list to less than twenty names. After I have traded them for some time I will be familiar with their behaviours. Some of them are more volatile during the day than others. Some of them are up when there seems to be no leading sector in the market, and down when the overall market is up. You can have your own preferred list of companies, but these companies should be big cap, or at least medium cap stocks. In general, the movement of big cap stocks follow the movement of the market, and therefore when the day's market is positive, the chances for the big cap stocks of the leading sectors to go positive are quite likely.

On a triple digit loss day of the market, I might sit out and enjoy a day off by not buying and selling. Before the opening bell, the negative indexes futures and the news related to the other overseas markets will indicate that the market in North America will open in the negative direction. So the risk of losing can be avoided by not trading for the day. In a "down" market day, a stock could have the Day Low moving lower and lower as the day progresses, so buying near the Day Low might not be a smart move on that day! But it could be a buy opportunity on the next day if the market turns positive again.

There are books and courses that offer training on day trading. As a matter of fact, I have not read any such books or attained any courses related to day trading. I am not trying to compare my ways with the *other* day trading technique. What I am writing is from my own experience which I would like to share with you.

CHAPTER SIX

Simple Rules To Follow For Trading Stocks

I am not a stock wiz, and I am not very technical in analyzing stock charts to "predict" what the stock will perform in the future.

When I pick a particular stock during the

day, I do look at its day chart, five day chart, month chart, and year chart. These charts are readily available on the internet. The information on these charts does have some influence on my decision. But I am not in a hundred per cent "buy and hold" mode for this market, so a stock that shows a continuous growth in the year chart does not influence my decision not to sell the stock at the end of the day.

The day chart, five day chart, and month chart provide me some insight of the near future of the stock. For the big caps that I trade frequently, if a particular stock has a nice jump in the last three or four days for no particular reason, and if the market is taking a breather or stepping sideways on the following day, then this particular stock will likely be down because of profit-taking. If I do not own the stock, I will watch it if it has gone down below the price at which I had sold it the last time, and then I would consider buying it back again. If the five day chart of another stock is sloping upwards to the right and shows no signs of falling, and if

I do not own the stock, I might not chase it and wait till it comes down again some time later.

I prefer to trade between 10:30 a.m. and 3:30 p.m., and avoid buying within the first hour of the opening market and the last half hour before the market closes. I do not buy torpedo stocks (stocks that plummet sharply in a short time span); I do not buy Cinderella stocks (stocks that rise from pennies to $XY.00 in a very short period). I stick to the big cap companies.

I watch for ex-dividend dates of the big cap companies. I try to buy them a day before the ex-dividend dates and sell them on or after the ex-dividend dates. This way I can earn the dividend payout and if possible the gain by flipping the stocks.

Don't be too emotionally stuck with a particular stock or sector. Some people like airline companies because they like airplanes. Airline stocks are not the best equity to be owned these days. Some people like the high tech sector. Remember the high tech darling Nortel? I happened to own 2000 shares of Nortel in February 2001, and the company gave a very disappointing earnings guidance (I forgot on which day of the month) after the market was closed, on the following day the TSX (it was called TSE at that time) market was halted for a few hours due to very heavy trading of Nortel shares. My sell order was luckily filled at the end of the trading day, and my loss was close to $30,000, but at least I rescued $60,000 from the investment. If I hang on to it or average down the stock during the last few years, I could lose even more. I was glad that I made the decision to dump the stock, and I learned a very important lesson from this; sometimes it is necessary to cut the loss and move on. After that trade, I had not bought back the stock again. Even now in my Plan, I do not hold any high tech stocks; I trade RIM (Research in Motion) occasionally, but I do not hold it in the portfolio.

Don't buy a stock that has just gone through a reverse split. When a company continuously provides disappointing quarterly reports, I will avoid the risk of owning it. Avoid owning the stocks of companies that belong to a sector in trouble. The bank stocks were not good investments from October to December of 2008. I started to trade them from the beginning of 2009, but I keep my ears open for the news related to the banking industry, so that I could be nimble enough to react quickly. Here are some signs of troubles for stocks to slide: (1) watch for signals such as missing lowered forecast; (2) selling near the Lows; (3) stop giving earnings guidance; (4) dividend cuts; (5) stop repurchasing shares; (6) lack of diversification; and (7) troubled sector.

We all have our own target of investment returns. Some like to invest in GICs and government bonds for minimum risk. In the stock market, there is considerable risk but the return on investment is good for long term investing. In trading, we can also have quick targeted returns if we can minimize the risks by sticking to some disciplines. That is why I stress so many times that the trading should be limited to big cap stocks. Your risk of losing money will be smaller when you own them compared with those penny stocks. If you have to hang on to the big cap stocks for a short period of time, just be patient because of a temporary setback. If you own the stocks only during the trading hours, and sell them before the closing bell whenever possible, your risk of losing due to market falling the next morning will be minimized. You will consistently making cash gain in your portfolio, and the market value of your portfolio is less susceptible to a market downturn the next day.

Once you decide on your profit target, you should stick to it. Don't be greedy. If the stock you own hits your target price, especially during the first half hour after the market's opening bell, sell it; because you are not guaranteed that the stock will go higher later in the day. I've learned my lessons of seeing my gain turning into a loss during the day because I didn't sell to take the profit. After a stock has been sold, don't feel regretful if the stock continues to climb. You've already made a profit by selling it earlier and there are always chances that the same stock can be bought back at a lower price.

I like to caution you here about one thing. While you are placing an order, you must stay focus and avoid unnecessary distractions. I had made a few mistakes by entering the wrong number (100 instead of 1000) of shares in a sell order, or entering a lower sell price after making a quick calculation in my head, thinking that I could break-even or make a few dollars in a quick sell; well these mistakes had reduced my profits or made the trade into a loss. So it is always essential to do the trading with a clear mind and with concentration.

Chapter Seven

Your Equity Grows Under Your Watchful Eyes

In today's global economy, we do not know if there would be another economic tsunami which could be triggered by another crisis of some sort. The best you can do is to prepare yourself by taking control of your own financial future, and to build up some protection for your investment to avoid being a victim again if another crisis occurred. There is nothing that can provide you with a hundred per cent safety-proof system, so you have to raise your alert level at the same time while you are building up your assets. The first step you need to take is to learn how to make you equity grow under your watchful eyes.

You need an on-line discount trading account. There are a number of discount brokerage companies in the market. Choose the one that charges the commissions that you are willing to pay for each trade. In general, the discount trading companies charge you fewer commissions if the number of trades meets a minimum number within a specified time period. Initially you might have to pay a bit more, and then as your number of trades increases, the commissions will come down.

Buy big cap stocks, don't buy penny stocks. Therefore the amount of capital you need to setup in the trading account should be starting from around $50,000. The reason I pick this amount is that you can start trading with quantity of 500 shares or more for most big cap stocks. This account could be inside or outside the RRSP. There are pros and cons to trade inside or outside the RRSP; you have to weigh the pros and cons and make your decision.

You can treat this frequent trading like a business. For example, if you start with a capital of $200,000. The book value of all the stocks in your portfolio should be kept at around $100,000, and your operating cash should be kept at around $100,000 on the daily balance if possible. I am not a businessman, but I think this is a healthy model for running this business. The beauty of this business is: you are your own boss, and your overhead is very low, and you'll get paid from your gain in your portfolio. This business is one that you can start at home, and it does not require too much time to run it. As long as you are careful in what you are doing and you are not greedy, and with some degree of patience, you will make a profit. Your day's work could be finished before noon when your daily profit target is secured.

As I mentioned before, my capital was based on a monthly average cash balance of $95,400 in my RRSP. This is the cash that I use to trade stocks. With my Plan, I do not need to have the $900,000 requirement to retire as mentioned in Chapter 3, because all I need is around $96,000 in cash as capital to perform trading. My gain (less commission) in cash from trading is $42,323 in nine months, which is a 44% gain on the principal of $95,400. So give and take a few percentage points, I can say that my investment returns in nine months is 40%. (The total commissions for the nine months are approximately $5430; this is equivalent to an average of 4.3 trades per trading day in the nine month period.)

This is an excellent return rate if I could keep on going this way, and my target of making $50,000 cash return from trading for the twelve month period would be within reach. I told my Son Felix and his wife Stephanie that this was what I am doing, and they asked me if I could manage their accounts for them!

Chapter Eight

The Next Twenty-Five or More Years

My main source of retirement income will be from my RRSP by making periodic partial deregistration so that the money will supplement the other incomes from CPP and LIF, plus Old Age Security (OAS) when I reach 65. The only thing I do not like is every time I make the partial deregistration of the RRSP, I have to pay a percentage of tax to the government and an administrative fee to the brokerage company.

The CPP benefits are revised annually using the change in Consumer Price Index (CPI) over the last year; and OAS benefits are revised quarterly using the CPI for the previous quarter.

There is a claw back (or repayment) of the OAS benefits if my annual income was over $66,335 (this limit is for year 2009), so there is a disincentive to make too much partial deregistration of my RRSP each year. It seems that the government is regarding seniors to be too well off if their annual income exceeds $66,335, the OAS benefits that they are getting will be clawed back, meaning that for every extra dollar exceeding the $66,335 limit, seniors have to pay back a few nickels and dimes for every dollar received. If a senior's income is above $107,692, OAS benefits will be reduced to zero.

Until I am 71 (maybe this could be extended by the government later, as they have done so to extend it from age 69), when the RRSP has to be converted into a Registered Retirement Income Fund (RRIF), I will have 11 years (assuming that I will not die before I am 71) to trade stocks within my self-directed RRSP. I forecast that the RRSP account will have a conservative balance of $245,000 (the current market value balance is $300,000, assuming no gain or loss of the equity being held in the account, a cash income of $45,000 from trading of stocks per year, and a drawdown of $50,000 from the account each year for eleven years) when it will be converted into RRIF.

I plan to save $5,000 yearly into a Tax Free Savings Account (TFSA), so that in 11 years, I could build up the savings in the TFSA while at the same time using its balance for trading. Therefore when my self-directed RRSP will be converted into RRIF at 71, I still have a TFSA account to do trading.

It's hard to predict how long the retirement

investment amount will last in my Plan. There are a few variables such as how well I do in the RRSP, how much I take out per year from the RRSP before age 71, and what amount will be left in it when I reach the age of 71, how long this lump sum will last in the RRIF, and how much money I will have in the TFSA. But I am confident that from age 60 and beyond, I could live comfortably with the incomes from CPP, LIF, OAS, RRSP or RRIF (after 71), and TFSA.

Between age 60 and 65, I plan to drawdown from the RRSP approximately $50,000 per year. After my sixty-fifth birthday, I will receive the OAS benefits, and the drawdown from the RRSP per year could be reduced because of the income from the OAS benefits. From age 65 and beyond, I plan to maintain an average annual income near but not exceeding the income limit for OAS claw back.

I project that the RRIF and TFSA will conservatively have an amount of $245,000 and $55,000 respectively in year 2020 when I will be 71, and these two pots of money will be invested to supplement the combined annual income of approximately $18,000 from CPP, OAS and LIF. The annual income from the RRIF will be selected to pay $19,500 per year and will be exhausted in 2035. I will supplement these incomes with the income of $14,500 per year from the TFSA, assuming that my brain power is still well enough to allow me to do stock trading using the savings from the TFSA. To summarize, my income from age 72 onwards is around $52,000.

There is an alternate means of minimizing the drawdown of the RRSP each year between now and age 71. The drawdown of money from RRSP is subject to tax, and therefore if I can drawdown an annual amount that is equivalent to the total principal and interest paid for an investment loan, then I can trade stocks outside the RRSP using the investment loan. Before I retired, I had obtained an unsecured line of credit of $40,000 to be used for this if I elected to trade stocks outside the RRSP. The advantage of this is that interest for the investment loan is tax deductible. Profits from trading stocks outside the RRSP will be subjected to capital gains tax, but only 50% of the realized capital gains are taxed in Canada at an individual's tax rate. Another method of minimizing drawdown of the RRSP is to use the savings within the TFSA to trade stocks.

Based on the schemes mentioned above, the total drawdown of the RRSP will be reduced; a lower tax rate will apply to the income from capital gains of a straight trading account; capital gains tax does not apply to TFSA; and withdrawals from a TFSA is tax-free; and the overall annual income and tax payable will vary depends on different scenarios. If I am a software programmer, I might design a model to simulate different scenarios to optimize my annual net income and tax savings based on a mix of incomes derived from RRSP drawdown, from a straight trading account, and from the TFSA. The software simulation model could be a neat and challenging project to do.

There is one more thing that could affect the whole formula. I have not mentioned that I am capable and could consider taking part-time jobs if the money is right. I started my retirement at sixty, and I am just not quitting and doing nothing at all yet. There is still a demand in the job market that requires the unique skill set that I have.

CHAPTER NINE

Four Segments of 25 Years in Life

Some people say that the stock market is just like a casino. They invest in penny stocks with the mindset of hitting the jackpot. Just like you bring some money with you to a casino and do not have much high hope to come out with a big winning. Most people are willing to gamble away with their money in a casino, even knowing that the chance of winning is so remote. Some people might think that investing in the market is too risky and they stay absolutely away from it; and they prefer to keep their money in the bank's saving accounts.

In Michael Moore's latest movie, "Capitalism: A Love Story", Moore portrayed that the bad guys are big banks and hedge funds which "gambled" investors' money in complex derivatives that few, if any, really understood and which should be likened as betting in the casino. That's why I emphasized earlier in the book that I do not trade derivatives and I do not buy mutual funds any more.

In trading stocks, I think that the risks of losing are much less compared with going to the casino. The chance of winning in trading stocks is much, much higher than winning by gambling in a casino. Actually, I do not consider trading stocks in the market is like gambling in the casino at all. Occasionally, I like to go to the casino and feed my money into the slot machines. I just like the atmosphere and the feeling provided by the sights and sounds of the rows of slot machines.

We should not confuse trading stocks with gambling. We should not be obsessed with trading stocks either; therefore, we should exercise self-control on ourselves not to spend 24/7 in such activity. If we lose that self-control, we could be addicted to it. Like everything else in life, we should have a balance in what we are doing.

Once you have started trading frequently and have tasted some success, you might be gaining more confidence gradually and become bolder everyday. Trading stocks is serious business and should be treated as such. You should be proud of your success because this is a skill that you've developed, and your success is not due to luck. You are using your skill, instinct, and good judgement to make every trade a win for you.

My advice is, don't let your success put you into overdrive, or let your guards off and become too risk-taking. Stick to the business plan I described earlier. With some gain on-hand, you might be tempted to invest in penny stocks with your profit money. Stick with the big cap stocks!

My philosophy towards life is that a normal life span consists of four segments of 25 years. The first segment is growing up and prepare for the second 25 years. The second 25 year segment is building up wealth, and by choice, some people will start a family of their own. The third segment of 25 years should be a phase of gradual reducing responsibilities and obligations, and entering into retirement. In the third segment, we should be harvesting from our investment, but if we put a little bit of extra efforts in managing our portfolios, we could enhance the harvest amount; and this is exactly what I have written in the precious chapters of this book, and I am doing what I am preaching. The fourth (or final for most people) segment is a bonus if we live that long, but the important thing in old age is we need health and wealth to allow us to live in a dignified manner.

Happiness is to enjoy the results of good planning! Enjoy your controlled success and do not be greedy! Enjoy the progress you are making every day! Enjoy the achievement of reaching your financial goal! Share your experience with the people you know! Share your happiness with your family and friends!

CHAPTER TEN

Conclusion

This book was published approximately twelve months after the beginning of the worst economic recession since the Great Depression. It was written to tell my story of how I took control of my own financial future, after I had taken a twenty five per cent loss year over year of my investment portfolios, and turned my investment around to recover some of the loss by frequent trading of stocks. This recovery effort was very important to me because I planned to retire in the summer of 2009 when I reached 60.

I made the decision to retire because I had confidence that I could earn a high rate of return by trading stocks to supplement the retirement benefits from the CPP and another income from the LIF. Contrary to general belief that one requires to have a fortune in order to retire comfortably these days, I desired to retire and my retirement saving in the self-directed RRSP was about $214,000 in market value at that time. I didn't think of selling my house and use the equity to generate income for my retirement.

I use basic tools and simple rules for trading stocks in the RRSP; nothing fancy. The self-directed RRSP is held in a discount brokerage company; and the trading platform is a basic one without live streaming data. Of course, I need a PC at home to access the internet.

The rules that I apply are very simple. I only buy and sell big cap (or sometimes medium cap) stocks listed in the TSX, and I rarely buy/ sell U.S. stocks. In my RRSP portfolio, I try to maintain the cash balance at approximately $96,000 at the end of each month. During the day, I could use the cash balance to buy stocks as frequently as I want, but I make it a goal to sell the stocks at a profit on the same day. In case if the stocks were not sold, then I would try again in the next few days.

I always trade the same stocks from a list of ten to twenty big cap companies that represent different sectors of the market. I never trade penny stocks. My daily target was to earn $200 to $300 so that I could make about $5,000 per month based on 20 trading days in a month. This would not be difficult to achieve because I buy stocks in quantity of 1,000 and sell them at a price of $0.20 to $0.30 above the buy price.

If I could not sell the stocks at the end of the trading day, I would hang on to them because they were big cap stocks and their prices would eventually go up again. I make it a habit to listen and/or watch the business news in the morning before 9:30 so that I could know if the market would be in the positive or negative territory when it opens. For a triple digit loss day, I would sit out and not do any trading at all.

The picking and price entry point of a particular stock is the skill that one has to develop. I had shared my experience with you in Chapters 5 and 6. You could start trading with a cash capital of about $50,000; this amount would allow you to buy a quantity of 500 or more of most big cap and medium cap stocks. Your account should be held with roughly 50% stocks and 50% cash to reduce your risk of losing it all. The stocks that are being held must be big cap stocks. Your trading account could be inside or outside the RRSP.

At the time when I was writing this last chapter of the book, the return for a nine month period was about $42,000 of cash earnings based on a cash capital of about

$96,000. With three more months to go, this year's target of earning $50,000 would be achievable! My two years goal is to recover my loss of $100,000 due to the market meltdown.

No matter whether you are retired, soon-to-be retired, or at a younger age, if you are not happy with your financial adviser, or not happy with the performance of your portfolios, I suggest that you should take control of your financial future and start managing your own portfolios. You will be happy to see the instant results by trading stocks.

According to Statistics Canada, the average net worth of Canadian in the age group of 55 to 64 years is $407,417; so based on my philosophy for life, a normal life span could be made up of four segments of 25 years, we must work very hard during the second segment, and save for the winter like the Ant in the Aesop Fable of "The Ant and the Grasshopper".

For those working people who have some

kind of pension benefits from their employers, the retirement investment is held in a Locked-In Retirement Account (LIRA) or better known as a locked-in RRSP. LIRA is not insured or guaranteed; therefore the assets could decline due to poor investment performance. When retiring, owners of a LIRA may transfer to a LIF or purchase a life annuity. For example, if a person had been working for 40 years and had a LIRA with $300,000 in it, then it can be transferred to a LIF and could receive a maximum payment of $24,000 a year starting at age 65, but decreasing in payment every year and exhausting at age 87.

For my retirement, I have locked in $85,500 into a LIF, but for the rest of my retirement savings which is around $300,000 in the self-directed RRSP at the time when this book is written, I choose the higher degree of risk by trading stocks, which will give me higher returns for the next eleven years (from age 60 to 71). The advantages of implementing my Plan are: (1) I can retire earlier at age 60; (2) the drawdown on the self-directed RRSP for my retirement income is supported by the money made from trading stocks; and (3) the trading activity helps to keep my mind sharp at all times! My trading technique is not aggressive, and my self-imposed disciplines could reduce the risks of failures or minimize the probability of losing the entire investment.

In conclusion, I am full of confidence that my retired life will not be boring. It gives me great pleasure to begin my retirement and write my first book to share the experience with you!

ABBRIVIATIONS AND ACRONYMS

CAP   Capitalization

CPP   Canada Pension Plan

CPI   Consumer Price Index

DBPP   Defined Benefit Pension Plan

DCPP   Defined Contribution Pension Plan

DJIA   Dow Jones Industrial Average

EST   Eastern Standard Time

ETF   Exchange Traded Fund

GDP   Gross Domestic Product

GIC   Guaranteed Investment Certificate

LIF   Life Income Fund

LIRA   Locked-In Retirement Account

M&A   Mergers and Acquisitions

OAS   Old Age Security

PC   Personal Computer

RRIF   Registered Retirement Income Fund

RRSP   Registered Retirement Savings Plan

S&P   Standards and Poor

TFSA   Tax Free Savings Account

TSE   Toronto Stock Exchange

TSX   Toronto Stock Exchange

Notes

Notes

Notes

Notes

Notes

Notes

Notes

Notes

www.ingramcontent.com/pod-product-compliance
Lightning Source LLC
Chambersburg PA
CBHW022102170526
45157CB00004B/1444

* 9 7 8 1 4 2 6 9 2 0 1 1 0 *